AMAZING MACHINES

CRANES

BY QUINN M. ARNOLD

CREATIVE EDUCATION • CREATIVE PAPERBACKS

Published by Creative Education and Creative Paperbacks
P.O. Box 227, Mankato, Minnesota 56002
Creative Education and Creative Paperbacks are imprints of
The Creative Company
www.thecreativecompany.us

Design by The Design Lab
Production by Chelsey Luther
Art direction by Rita Marshall
Printed in the United States of America

Photographs by Alamy (Zoonar GmbH), Dreamstime (Berkut34,
Roman Milert, Somakram, Youths), Getty Images (SeongJoon Cho/
Bloomberg), iStockphoto (karp85), Shutterstock (Potapov Alexander,
Corepics VOF, Paula Fisher, E. G. Pors, pryzmat, James Steidl)

Library of Congress Cataloging-in-Publication Data
Names: Arnold, Quinn M., author.
Title: Cranes / Quinn M. Arnold.
Series: Amazing machines.
Includes bibliographical references and index.
Summary: A basic exploration of the parts, variations, and worksites
of cranes, the tall moving machines. Also included is a pictorial
diagram of variations of cranes.
Identifiers: ISBN 978-1-60818-888-8 (hardcover) / ISBN 978-1-
62832-504-1 (pbk) / ISBN 978-1-56660-940-1 (eBook)
This title has been submitted for CIP processing under LCCN
2017937612.

CCSS: RI.1.1, 2, 4, 5, 6, 7; RI.2.2, 5, 6, 7, 10; RI.3.1, 5, 7, 8;
RF.1.1, 3, 4; RF.2.3, 4

First Edition HC 9 8 7 6 5 4 3 2 1
First Edition PBK 9 8 7 6 5 4 3 2 1

Table of Contents

Cranes are tall machines. They lift and lower heavy objects. Wooden cranes were used thousands of years ago. The first metal crane was made in 1834. Most cranes today are made of strong steel.

The first metal crane was made of cast iron and powered by hand.

The shorter beam behind the cab is the counter-jib.

The **mast** stands tall. A long beam, or jib, is near the top. Some cranes have a **trolley**. This runs along the jib. It moves the load where it needs to go.

mast the vertical part of the crane; also known as the boom

trolley a cart that moves along rails

Wires are twisted together to make rope-like cables.

Cables hang down from the crane. Hooks, magnets, or buckets are attached to the cables. They are raised and lowered by **pulleys**. A part called a counterweight keeps the crane from tipping.

pulleys systems of small wheels used with ropes, chains, or cables to move heavy objects

There are many different types of cranes. Some can lift up to 20 tons (18.1 t). Gantry cranes may lift more than 20,000 tons (18,144 t)! These cranes have two masts. They move on rails. They help build and repair ships.

Some gantry cranes load and unload container ships.

Floating cranes are on special boats. These cranes help build bridges and oil rigs. Sometimes they even recover sunken ships.

A flat-bottomed barge may carry a small floating crane.

Crawler cranes can move over rough ground on their wide treads.

The base of a tower crane bolts into a large concrete pad. It stays in one place. But some cranes can move. Crawler cranes move around on **caterpillar treads**. Other cranes are attached to big trucks.

caterpillar treads bands looped around roller wheels to help heavy vehicles move

A crane operator sits in the cab. Foot pedals and joysticks control the crane. These swing the jib left and right. They move the trolley and the pulley. A person on the ground helps the operator place the load.

A part called the slewing ring helps make a tower crane spin.

Tower cranes often work on construction sites. They lift large beams to build the tallest buildings. They move heavy objects around the site.

A tower crane has to be put together again every time it moves sites.

Tall cranes lift heavy loads. They help build and tear down structures. Look for a crane the next time you see a worksite. Watch what the heavy machine is lifting!

Cranes work on buildings that are hundreds of feet tall.

Crane Blueprint

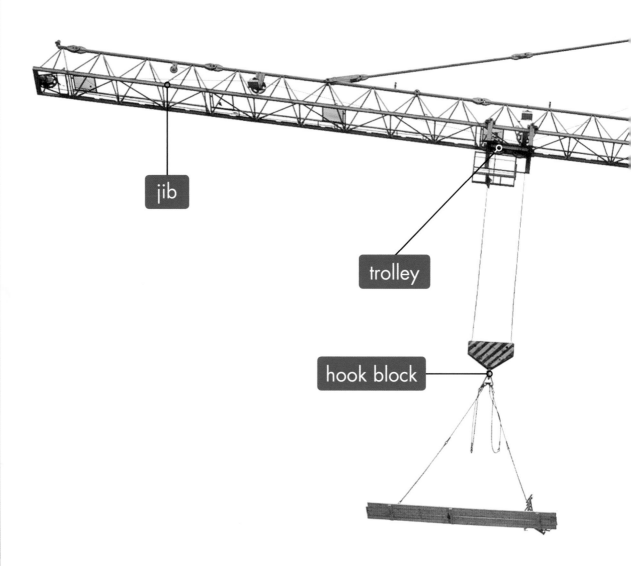

jib

trolley

hook block

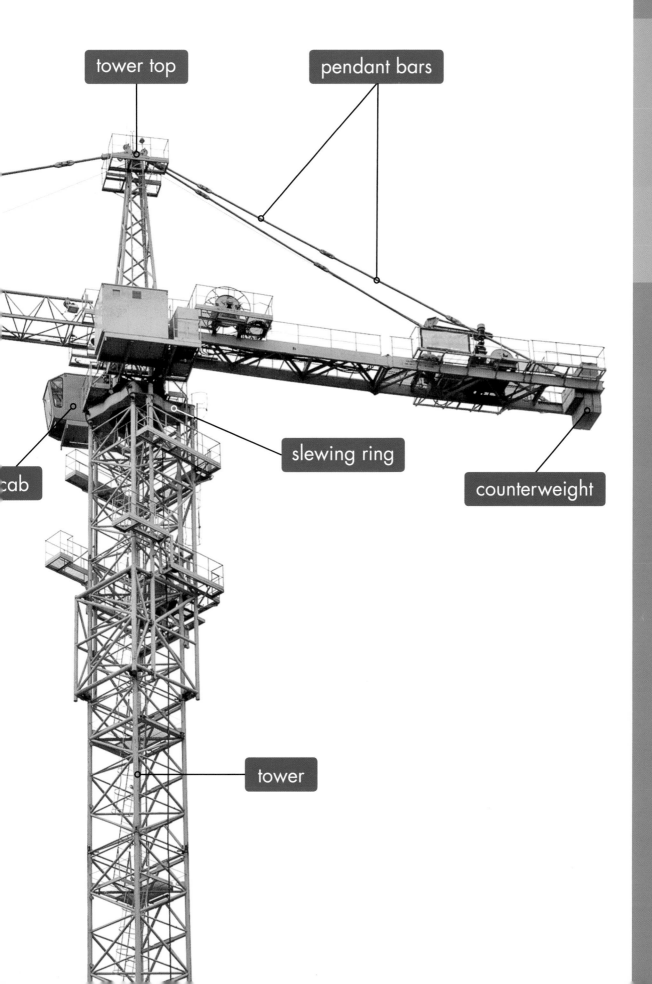

tower top

pendant bars

cab

slewing ring

counterweight

tower

Read More

Allen, Kenny. *Giant Cranes*. New York: Gareth Stevens, 2013.

Bowman, Chris. *Cranes*. Minneapolis: Bellwether Media, 2017.

Schuh, Mari. *Cranes*. North Mankato, Minn.: Amicus, 2018.

Websites

Dismantling the World's Largest Tower Crane
https://www.youtube.com/watch?v=hUyLQ8OR7Vw
Watch a video of a tower crane disassembly.

PBS Kids: Build
http://pbskids.org/designsquad/build/heavy-lifting/
Follow the instructions to build and test your own crane.

Note: Every effort has been made to ensure that the websites listed above are suitable for children, that they have educational value, and that they contain no inappropriate material. However, because of the nature of the Internet, it is impossible to guarantee that these sites will remain active indefinitely or that their contents will not be altered.

Index